IT'S RAINING!

DISCARD

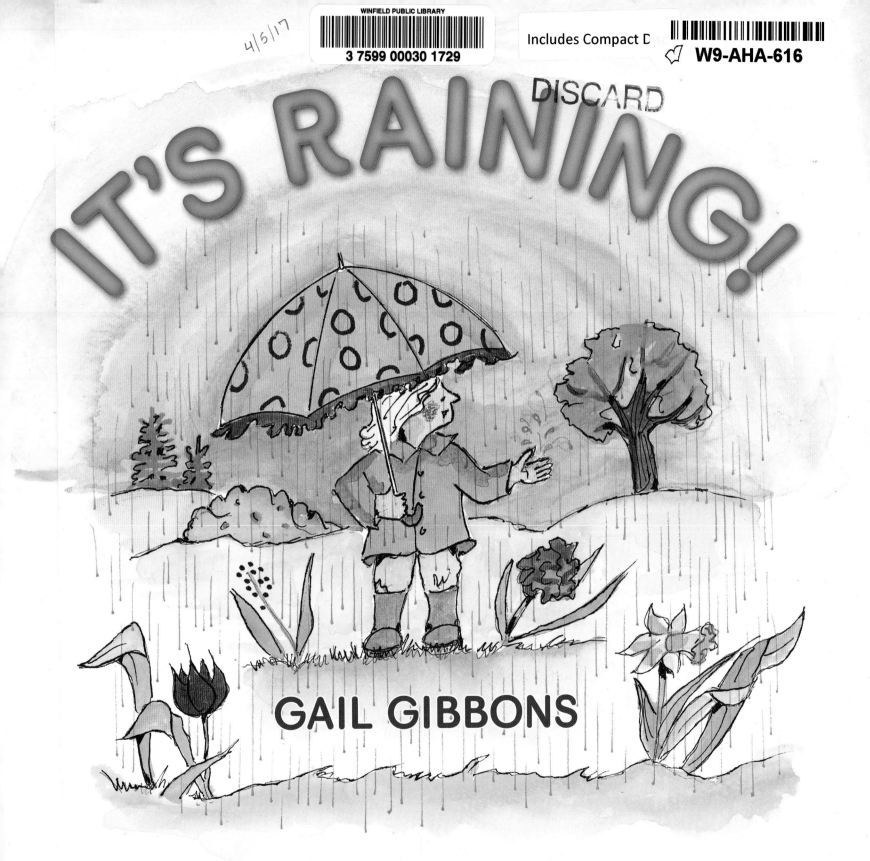

GAIL GIBBONS

Holiday House / New York

To Kathleen and Maury Colton

Special thanks to Eric Evenson of
the National Weather Service
South Burlington, Vermont.

HOLIDAY HOUSE is registered in the
U.S. Patent and Trademark Office.
Printed and Bound in June 2015
at Toppan Leefung, DongGuan City, China.
www.holidayhouse.com
3 5 7 9 10 8 6 4

Library of Congress Cataloging-in-Publication Data
Gibbons, Gail, author, illustrator.
It's raining! / by Gail Gibbons. — First edition.
pages cm
Summary: "A thorough explanation of the
formation and effects of rain."
— Provided by publisher.
Audience: 4-8.
Audience: Pre-school.
ISBN 978-O-8234-2924-O (hardcover)
1. Rain and rainfall—Juvenile literature.
2. Meteorology—Juvenile literature.
I. Title. II. Title: It is raining!
QC924.7.G53 2014
551.57'7—dc23

ISBN 978-O-8234-33O3-2 (paperback)

Dark clouds fill the sky. Some people pull on boots and put on raincoats and hats. Others pop open umbrellas. It's raining!

Rain is water falling from clouds. Water is necessary for all plant life...

and animal life to survive on Earth.

THE WATER CYCLE

THE CONSTANT MOVEMENT OF MOISTURE ON EARTH

WATER VAPOR is made up of very tiny particles of water that we cannot see.

When the sun shines and warms the air, water vapor rises up into the sky. This is called evaporation.

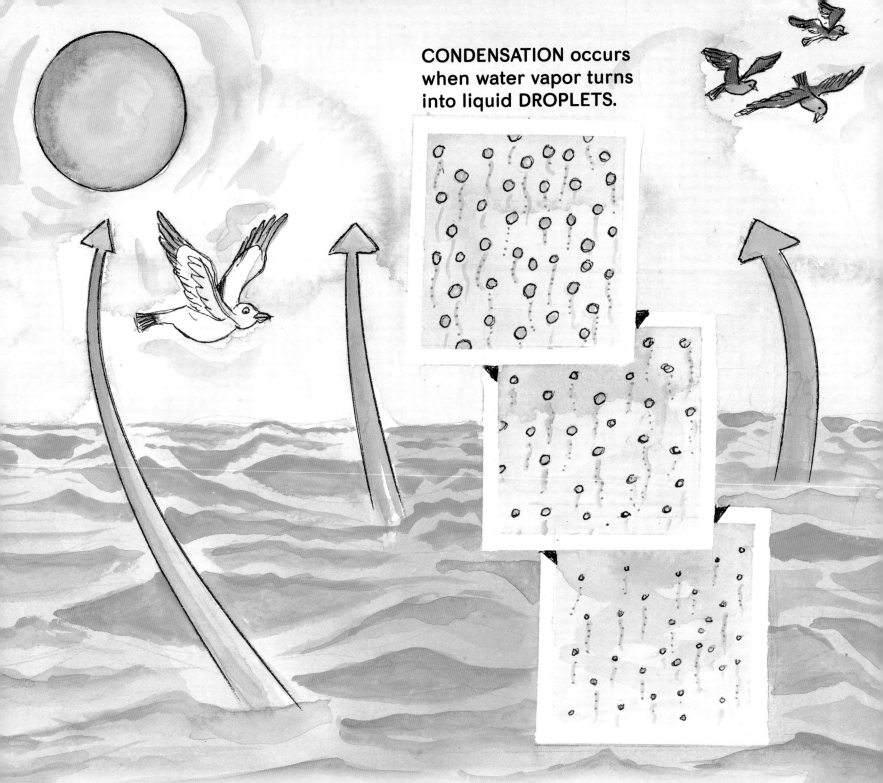

CONDENSATION occurs
when water vapor turns
into liquid DROPLETS.

As the water vapor moves higher into the sky, the air
becomes cooler and cooler. Water vapor soon turns into
millions of water droplets. This is called condensation.

CLOUDS

CLOUDS

DROPLETS

Clouds will form when enough droplets come together.

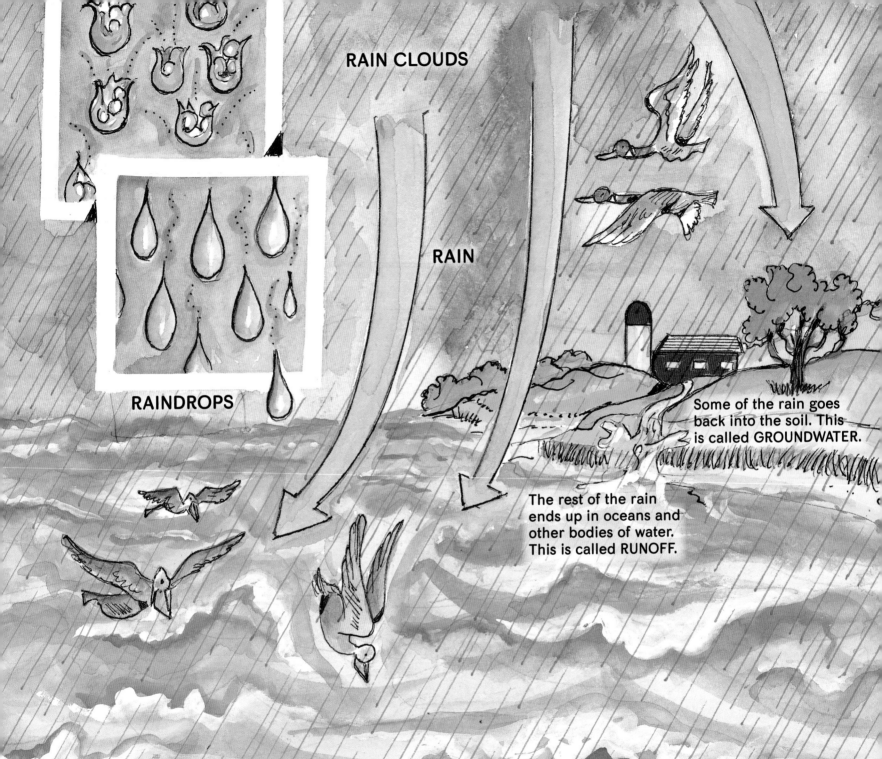

RAIN CLOUDS

RAINDROPS

RAIN

Some of the rain goes back into the soil. This is called GROUNDWATER.

The rest of the rain ends up in oceans and other bodies of water. This is called RUNOFF.

As droplets join together, they become heavy enough to fall toward Earth as raindrops.

DIFFERENT KINDS OF RAIN CLOUDS

STRATUS RAIN CLOUDS

Stratus clouds produce drizzle or light rain and are low in the sky. They are spread out across the entire sky.

NIMBOSTRATUS RAIN CLOUDS

Nimbostratus clouds are dark and bring steady, heavy rain. When clouds look dark to us it is because there are so many water droplets in the clouds that the rays of the sun can't shine through.

CUMULUS RAIN CLOUDS

STRATOCUMULUS CLOUDS

ALTOCUMULUS CLOUDS

Stratocumulus and altocumulus clouds produce drizzle or light rain. They are patchy, puffy clouds low in the sky.

CUMULONIMBUS RAIN CLOUDS

Cumulonimbus clouds can be taller than 60,000 feet (18,288 meters) in the sky.

Cumulonimbus clouds are dark, heavy, and piled up high in the sky. These large clouds bring lots of rain.

WHERE IT RAINS IN NORTH AMERICA ...

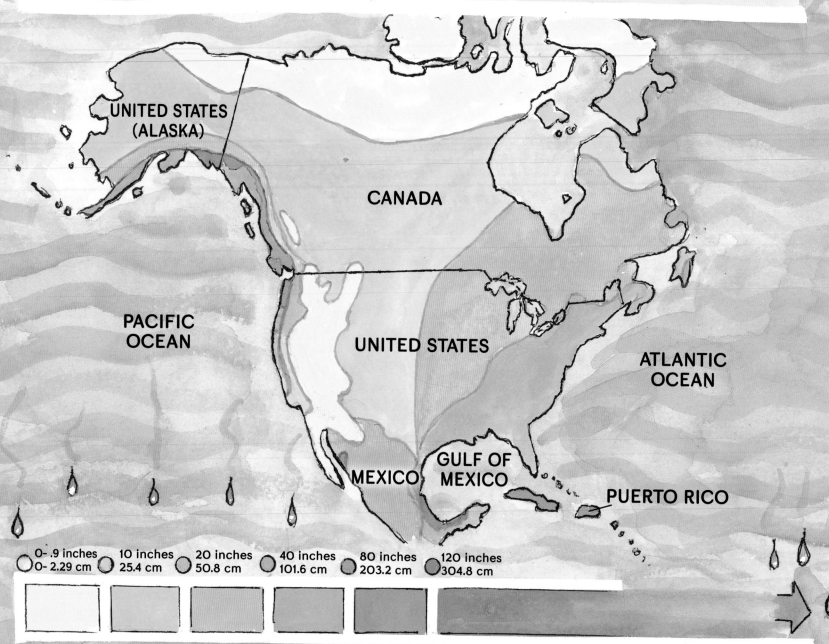

UNITED STATES (ALASKA)

CANADA

PACIFIC OCEAN

UNITED STATES

ATLANTIC OCEAN

MEXICO

GULF OF MEXICO

PUERTO RICO

| ○ 0- .9 inches
○ 0- 2.29 cm | ○ 10 inches
○ 25.4 cm | ○ 20 inches
○ 50.8 cm | ○ 40 inches
○ 101.6 cm | ○ 80 inches
○ 203.2 cm | ○ 120 inches
○ 304.8 cm |

YEARLY AVERAGE RAINFALL

The amount of rainfall during a year varies from place to place all around North America.

AND AROUND THE WORLD

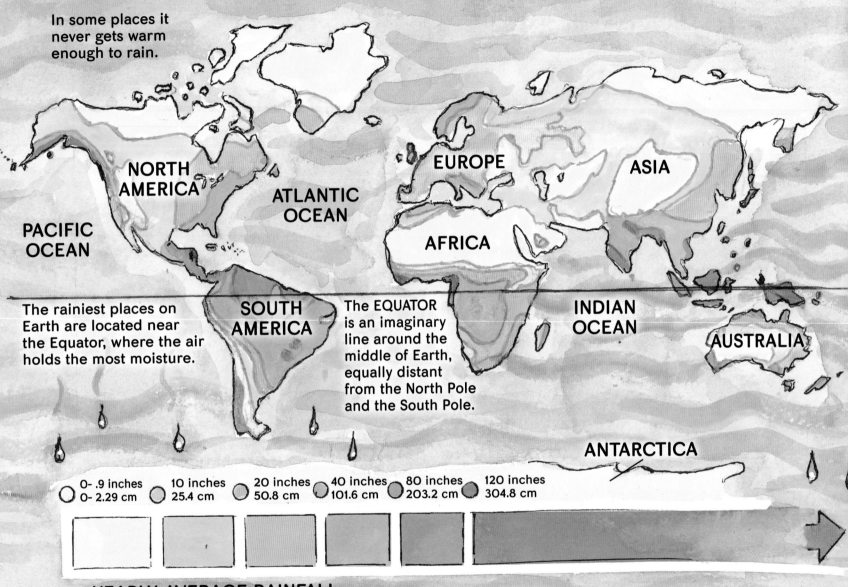

In some places it never gets warm enough to rain.

NORTH AMERICA

ATLANTIC OCEAN

PACIFIC OCEAN

EUROPE

ASIA

AFRICA

The rainiest places on Earth are located near the Equator, where the air holds the most moisture.

SOUTH AMERICA

The EQUATOR is an imaginary line around the middle of Earth, equally distant from the North Pole and the South Pole.

INDIAN OCEAN

AUSTRALIA

ANTARCTICA

0- .9 inches	10 inches	20 inches	40 inches	80 inches	120 inches
0- 2.29 cm	25.4 cm	50.8 cm	101.6 cm	203.2 cm	304.8 cm

YEARLY AVERAGE RAINFALL

Rain helps determine the kinds of plant life in all regions of the world. It also helps create the level of water in streams, rivers, lakes, and oceans.

RAIN FALLS FROM CLOUDS IN DIFFERENT WAYS.

DRIZZLE

STRATOCUMULUS RAIN CLOUDS

When very small raindrops are falling lightly, people say, "It's drizzling!"

SHOWER

ALTOCUMULUS RAIN CLOUDS

If the sun shines during a shower, we call this a sun shower.

A shower occurs when the raindrops are larger than drizzle. A shower lasts for a short amount of time.

RAIN

NIMBOSTRATUS RAIN CLOUDS

Everyone tries to get out of the rain.

Rain occurs when the raindrops are large and come down steadily.

18

RAINSTORM

CUMULONIMBUS RAIN CLOUDS

CAUTION!
STAY AWAY FROM WINDOWS.

Tree branches can get knocked down.

A rainstorm is when there are gusty winds and rain comes down for a long time.

THUNDERSTORM

People try to stay safe indoors.

CUMULONIMBUS RAIN CLOUDS

People cover their windows to protect themselves from flying glass and other objects.

During a thunderstorm it gets dark and windy. Raindrops come down hard and fast.

LIGHTNING is a flash
of electricity.

When raindrops bump against one
another violently, they make electricity.

Lightning is so hot that the particles
of water vapor in the air around it
expand. BOOM!!! The powerful
noise is called THUNDER.

Thunderstorms can be very dangerous! There is thunder
and lightning.

FLASH FLOOD

ALERT!

METEOROLOGISTS are scientists who study and predict the weather.

A RAIN GAUGE measures the amount of rainfall. The information is downloaded by meteorologists onto their computers.

A FLASH FLOOD is rapid and sudden flooding usually caused by heavy rain.

Sometimes meteorologists warn people of an approaching storm and possible flooding. A flood can bring great danger.

To EVACUATE means to leave the area. People are told to move to safer places.

EVACUATION ROUTE

SHELTER

Some people go to shelters. A SHELTER is a place where people go to be safe until they can return home.

Floodwaters can rise quickly. People living near streams, rivers, and lakes are sometimes advised by meteorologists and authorities to evacuate.

Power lines are repaired.

Damaged trees and branches are cut up and taken away.

After a major rainstorm or flash flood has passed, there often is damage. Cleanup crews get busy.

Workers and volunteers come together as cleanup teams.

Roads may be washed away.

SAFETY LINES

Homes and buildings may need repairs.

25

The use of gasoline, oil, and coal adds pollutants to the air.

When strong pollutants in the air come down with the rain, it is called acid rain. Acid rain can cause damage to trees, crops, and all living things.

HYDRO POWER is created from the movement of water.

WIND POWER is created from the movement of the wind.

SOLAR POWER is created from the heat of the sun.

Without clean water, plants and crops may die. People and animals suffer too. Many people are looking at new forms of energy such as hydro power, wind power, and solar power to help cut back on pollution.

Sometimes while it's raining or just after it's rained there is . . .

The order of the
colors of the rainbow
is always the same.

RAINBOW

a RAINBOW!

HOW TO STAY DRY OUTSIDE WHEN IT RAINS . . .

UMBRELLA

HAT

PONCHO

JACKET

RAIN BOOTS

RUBBER SHOES

HOW TO STAY SAFE DURING A THUNDERSTORM

When there is lightning, never stand near or under a tree. The tree and its roots will carry and transfer electricity that can hurt anything near them.

Don't swim in water out of doors. Water attracts lightning.

As soon as possible take cover inside your house or a large building.

HOW TO STAY SAFE INSIDE DURING A THUNDERSTORM OR A FLOOD

Make sure you are in a safe place with an adult.

Bring your pets inside.

Listen to weather forecasters to be on alert.

Stay away from windows and doors.

When there is lightning, stay away from anything that can transfer electricity, such as water faucets or electrical appliances.

MAKE SURE YOU HAVE . . .

FRESH WATER
BATTERY-POWERED RADIO
FIRST AID KIT
SPARE BATTERIES
NONPERISHABLE FOODS
FLASHLIGHT

RAIN . . . RAIN . . . RAIN . . .

Fog is a stratus cloud close to the ground.

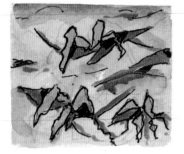

A drought happens when it hasn't rained for a long time. There is no water, so plants can't grow.

Monsoons are extra heavy seasonal rains that fall mostly in Southeast Asia. As much as one foot (.3m) or more of rain per hour can fall during a monsoon.

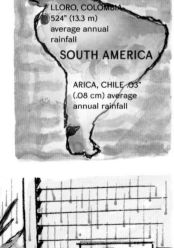

LLORO, COLOMBIA 524" (13.3 m) average annual rainfall

SOUTH AMERICA

ARICA, CHILE .03" (.08 cm) average annual rainfall

Both the place with the highest annual rainfall and the place with the lowest annual rainfall around the world are found in South America.

Freezing rain is very dangerous. When warm raindrops fall and hit cold surfaces, ice forms. Streets and sidewalks become slippery; electrical wires can snap. There is danger everywhere.

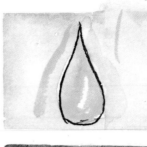

Each raindrop is made up of about a million droplets.

Throughout the world, there are about sixteen million thunderstorms a year.

Count the seconds between a flash of lightning and a clap of thunder. The bigger the number, the farther away the storm is.

A rainbow is an arc of seven different colors. It forms when sunlight shines through drops of water.

WEBSITES:

United States
www.nws.noaa.gov

Canada
http://weather.gc.ca/
canada_e.html